People often ask me, "If you could be any kind of animal, what would you be?" I usually say I'd like to be a huge grizzly bear, so I could kill people who ask stupid questions.

If you're a huge grizzly bear, you don't have to feel guilty about slaying the idiots around you because it's a totally natural thing. But if you're unlucky enough to be among nature's least powerful creatures—"employees"—then you'll need different strategies to survive. I recommend mocking your coworkers behind their backs. It's not as satisfying as killing them with your huge claws, but it takes less energy. And I think that's something we can all appreciate.

There are many other ideas in this book—every one of them at least as good as the advice you got in the introduction. I'm here to help.

S. Adams

ISBN: 0-8362-3224-0

PLEASE DON'T FEED THE **EGOS**

And Other Tips for Corporate Survival

A DILBERT™ BOOK
BY
SCOTT ADAMS

Andrews McMeel
Publishing

Kansas City

TEAMWORK MAY BE HAZARDOUS TO YOUR HEALTH.

9/12/96 © United Feature Syndicate, Inc. (NYC)

CASUAL DAY IS NO TIME TO MAKE FASHION STATEMENTS.

6/2/95 © United Feature Syndicate, Inc. (NYC)

8/9/95 © United Feature Syndicate, Inc. (NYC)

2/9/94 © United Feature Syndicate, Inc. (NYC)

BEWARE THE FURY OF UNDERPAID CLERICAL WORKERS.

12/14/95 © United Feature Syndicate, Inc. (NYC)

HEY, WALLY, HOW DID YOU GET A ROOF FOR YOUR CUBICLE?

THIS STUFF IS ALL MODULAR. YOU JUST TAKE SOME IDIOT'S WALL AND MAKE IT YOUR CEILING.

BY ANY CHANCE, DO YOU KNOW WHAT HAPPENED TO MY WALL?

WHAT DID IT LOOK LIKE?

2/19/93 © United Feature Syndicate, Inc. (NYC)

WHERE ARE YOU TAKING ALL OF THAT OFFICE EQUIPMENT?

I'M HAVING A GARAGE SALE.

THERE IS NO CONNECTION BETWEEN YOUR WORK AND YOUR PAY.

2/15/95 © United Feature Syndicate, Inc. (NYC)

9/15/95 © United Feature Syndicate, Inc. (NYC)

11/23/94 © United Feature Syndicate, Inc. (NYC)

PLEASE DON'T FEED THE EGOS.

9/7/95 © United Feature Syndicate, Inc. (NYC)

9/8/95 © United Feature Syndicate, Inc. (NYC)

HERE'S MY TIME SHEET, INCLUDING GUESSES FOR THE NEXT TWO DAYS SO I CAN MEET YOUR ARBITRARY CLERICAL DEADLINE.

IF ANYTHING IMPORTANT COMES UP, I'LL IGNORE IT TO PRESERVE THE INTEGRITY OF THE TIME-REPORTING SYSTEM.

ARE YOU FINISHED ANNOYING ME YET?

ACCORDING TO MY TIME SHEET I'LL BE HERE FOR ANOTHER 14 MINUTES.

HATE LL OF MY O-WORKERS.

DESPITE THE NAME, FOOD STAMPS ARE NOT EDIBLE.

4/23/96 © United Feature Syndicate, Inc. (NYC)

YOUR BIG MISTAKE, EVOLUTION-WISE, WAS INVENTING COMPUTERS THAT ARE EASIER TO USE IF YOU HAVE A TAIL.

IT'S AN IRONIC TWIST IN THE DARWINIAN SAGA. YOU'VE GUARAN- TEED THE EXTINC- TION OF YOUR OWN SPECIES.

STOP WORKING WHILE I'M TALKING TO YOU, ZIMBU!!

I CAN HEAR THE EVOLUTIONARY CLOCK ... TICK- TICK-TICK-TICK

EVOLUTION FAVORS MONKEYS. EVENTUALLY, HUMANS WILL BE KEPT IN CAGES AS PETS

BAH!

3/31/94 © United Feature Syndicate, Inc. (NYC)

BEWARE

THE COMPETITION OF CREATURES WHO ARE ACCUSTOMED TO CRUEL LAB EXPERIMENTS.

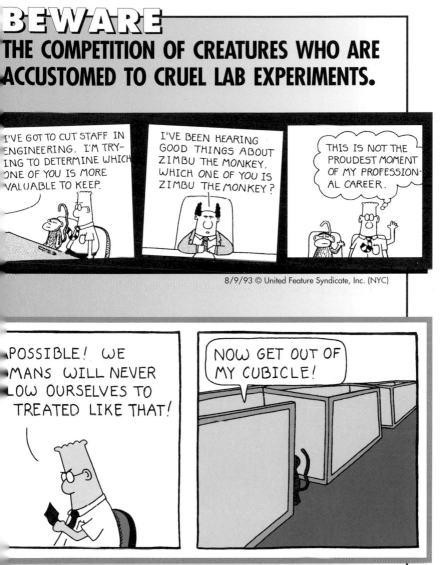

8/9/93 © United Feature Syndicate, Inc. (NYC)

4/1/94 © United Feature Syndicate, Inc. (NYC)

I DON'T UNDERSTAND WHY SOME PEOPLE WASH THEIR BATH TOWELS.

WHEN I GET OUT OF THE SHOWER I'M THE CLEANEST OBJECT IN MY HOUSE. IN THEORY, THOSE TOWELS SHOULD BE GETTING CLEANER EVERY TIME THEY TOUCH ME.

MAYBE I COULD HUG YOU EVERY DAY SO I DON'T NEED TO TAKE SHOWERS.

ARE TOWELS SUPPOSED TO BEND?

SHOULD I GIVE YOU CPR?

NO-O-O-O!! LET ME DIE!!

11/24/95 © United Feature Syndicate, Inc. (NYC)

I NEED THIS INFORMATION TODAY. PLUS A COMPLETE ANALYSIS OF THE ALTERNATIVES.

CRINKLE
CRINKLE
STUFF

THAT WASN'T NICE.

IN TODAY'S LESSON, YOU LEARN THAT YOU'RE MY CO-WORKER, NOT MY BOSS.

5/30/96 © United Feature Syndicate, Inc. (NYC)

AS YOU KNOW, I'VE BEEN PROMOTED TO TEAM LEADER.

NEVER CONFUSE RESPONSIBILITY WITH POWER.

9/28/95 © United Feature Syndicate, Inc. (NYC)

1/23/95 © United Feature Syndicate, Inc. (NYC)

UNLESS YOU ENJOY PHYSICAL PAIN, REFRAIN FROM SAYING ANYTHING THAT MAY BE CONSTRUED AS SEXIST.

5/1/96 © United Feature Syndicate, Inc. (NYC)

3/27/95 © United Feature Syndicate, Inc. (NYC)

I DIDN'T REALIZE YOU HAD COFFEE WENCHES IN THIS COUNTRY TOO.

CONTINUED...

I HOPE YOU DON'T WANT CHILDREN, YORGI.

DILBERT, I'M SENDING YOU TO "DIVERSITY SENSITIVITY" TRAINING.

ALICE DOESN'T HAVE TO GO BECAUSE CHICKS ARE BORN ALREADY KNOWING THIS STUFF. IT'S AS NATURAL AS SHOPPING AND CRYING.

CAN I GET A "MIDOL" FOR EITHER ONE OF YOU?

WHUMP WHUMP WHUMP

5/31/94 © United Feature Syndicate, Inc. (NYC)